C000212150

# Finding Work In Spain

## *"Living In Spain Series"* Book 2

*By David Wright*

Copyright © 2012 Author Name

ISBN:
ISBN-13: 9781729021156

# Table Of Contents

# INTRODUCTION.

*This book was written to help others learn* **How To Find Work In Spain.**

All info is based on my personal experiences and views, the information could be subject to change at any time and although I try to keep the information here updated things are changing with Brexit fast and you should always get professional legal help when moving to Spain.

David has lived and worked in Spain for 16 years now and worked for other people and companies as well as being self employed and running  his own building and carpentry business here and over the years has employed all nationalities.

When first here David worked mostly for British expats here refurbishing their properties and this included bars and restaurants. Then he went self employed and did work for himself mostly but on occasions worked for many other larger companies including the local Spanish government offices and buildings

In this book David will outline just what he did to find **work in Spain** and things that you need to do to give yourself the best chance of a good job in Spain. Whether you speak Spanish or not there are ways that you can find *work in Spain* if you follow his tips and advice.

There is work in Spain for those who speak Spanish and those who don't speak Spanish.

At the bottom of some chapters We have included reference

links to info that David has used personally or has been recommended to him by friends here.

There are many people who **move to Spain** for a better way of life but once here they find that they need to work, part time or full time but they do struggle with finding work so these tips and advice accumulated over 16 years of living and working here should help your chances greatly of **Finding Work In Spain**.

# ABOUT THE AUTHOR.

**David Charles Wright**, is an English man, born in 1962, who became frustrated and disillusioned with the rat race 9 to 5 way of life and poor weather in the Uk, so 16 years ago followed his dream and made the move to sunny Spain in search of a better way of life.

Going through a divorce and a global crisis that hit Spain hard he has survived both and now married to Llani a Spanish girl for over 5 years he has extensive knowledge and contacts on both sides of life, first as a British expat and from a Spanish resident with a Spanish wife and large Spanish family.

David has traveled all over Spain with his Spanish wife and to more than 20 other countries around the world including recently his dream destination of Bora Bora and Tahiti in the south Pacific and they still travel regularly but has now stopped working on his own building business and bought a plot of land here to start his next major project of building his dream 4 bedroom villa here in Spain.

In the 16 years David has lived and worked here, he has made some valuable work contacts that he shares in links throughout this book as he wishes others to have a smoother transition to their new life in sunny Spain.

David has built up a very useful list of contacts all over Spain from trades professionals and estate agents all the way up to being personal friends with the chief of the British consulate here in Almeria. You can now get access to all his contacts right here.

# CHAPTER 1

## *Even Before You Move Here*

*Even before you move to Spain there is so much that you can do about finding* **work in Spain** *that costs nothing, just your time.*

*Over the years I have seen so many people* **move to Spain** *in search of a better way of life and I have seen personally many of these people fail here and return to the UK with next to nothing. I have now started writing a few books on things that I have seen that you should and should not do to make your stay in Spain a long and successful one.*

*At first Seeing People move here and fail just made me think how ignorant they were for not looking into it more and not being prepaid but I feel a little sad too as I know what it is like to have a dream to move to Spain, so now writing these books may provide them with all the information in one place that can help them make a better informed decision before things start going wrong.*

*Research is key here and you can never do too much of it especially when it comes to moving to a new country even though it's just a few hours away by plane.*

*The internet will get you started, but where do you start?*

*If you are thinking of moving to Spain that's great, I too had that dream 16 years ago, but where is your ideal place and what parts of Spain do you like?*

*Is it sandy beaches or the country or mountains? This may have a big affect on your chances of finding work in Spain.*

**Also what sort of work are you after and do you speak Spanish?**

Probably the number 1 reason why people fail at fin**ding work in Spain** or a good job in Spain, is that they don't bother to learn Spanish. You still can find work here if you don't speak Spanish but it will limit your options and wages .

*In this book I will give examples of work and jobs that you can find for those who do speak Spanish and for those who Don't speak Spanish.*

*Let's start off and say that you like the sandy beaches and areas near the coast. Ok so if you don't speak Spanish then you will need to go where there are English speakers and these are places like Benidorm where there are 70,000 British people living now.*

*Alicantes area of Torrevieja has 18,000 British people.*

*Javea has 32,000 British, Benalmadena has 17,000. Murcia now has over 7,500 British.*

*Malaga has more than 16,000 British. Barcelona has 6,000 British and growing fast.*

*There are many more places like this that are mostly in the larger more populated tourist areas but these are the places that you need and more likely to Find Work In Spain if you don't speak Spanish.*

*These are also great areas if you do speak Spanish as a lot of these British will just have moved here so may be in need of your services here.*

*If your Spanish is ok then you may want to live in the country or hills of Spain, maybe a place out of the way and a bit quieter. If this is the case then you will mostly be working for Spanish people because if there are Brits there they will be fewer and more spread out.*

*There are a few English companies here who are employing British people who don't speak any Spanish but these are nearly always near the coast of in big cities.*

*Research is key now and even before you move to Spain you must think hard about location and this may not be a place that you really want to move to at first but may be the place where you have the best chances of finding work in Spain. You can always move on to the place you love once you have your foot in the door and found some work.*

*Once you start to work here for a while you will find and gain access to other jobs or work contacts that you may not ever find if you are not working here.*

## Example 1.

*A few years back a guy who has become a friend now moved here from London and didn't speak any Spanish so he started working a few one off jobs for a few of the British expats in the area doing odd jobs on their cars. After about 1 year he started to speak some Spanish and found a part time job working for a local Spanish garage as a fitter just changing car tires. Then they gave him a full time job with a contract. He really wants to live in Barcelona and in a few years he will move there as he will be able to speak better Spanish and get a job with a Spanish garage not just work for the Brits.*

## Example 2.

*There was a family that moved here a few years ago and they had a daughter who was about 30 that came with them. She had no work as she was part disabled with a leg problem. She was giving some local kids some private English lessons at home about 3 nights a week just to bring in a few Euros and then one of the kids teachers at school contacted her and asked if she would be interested in coming into the school 2 afternoons a week to just speak to the kids so as they could practice their English. She jumped at this offer and now works at the school almost every afternoon one way or another.*

*The biggest thing that you can do even before you move to Spain is start learning Spanish. Now you will hear me say this many times in all my books but it really is the number one thing that will change your chances of finding work in Spain.*

*There are local news papers and English speaking papers that are now online and these can be a great place to see just what jobs in Spain are on offer and where they are. Many British papers like the one near me have job offers and the local British community post work in these papers with contact numbers so you can get in touch with these people and see just what is involved and what sort of money they are paying.*

*These are local British papers publish here directed at the local British expats and some papers have huge followers now so these are well worth checking out and you can do it all from home in the uK.*

**Here are a few Local Newspapers in Spain that you can now read online from the comfort of your own home anywhere.**

**Some have sub links to other British news papers here in Spain.**

*The EuroWeekly News      based around the south of Spain..*

*https://www.euroweeklynews.com/classifieds/*

*Barcelona Metropolitan*

*https://www.barcelona-metropolitan.com/*

*Majorca Daily            https://majorcadailybulletin.com/*

*Spanish              sun              newspaper*
*http://www.spanishsunnewspaper.com/*

*Costa Blanca news*

*http://www.spain-newspaper.com/english-language.htm*

*There are many more just search online for the area that you like and there is nearly always a local British news paper there.*

*Also you could contact these papers and post your cv or add there and maybe even have a job interview set up before you move to Spain.*

*Just by spending some time each day online you can really get to know just what the job market is like in the area that you want to move to and even contact local people who are working there and send them an email asking what works like there and what they think you need to do first. Most times you will get a reply that could put a contact your way.*

*It's not always a good idea to go to Spain to look for work first time out, why not give yourself the best chance and do some good research even before you go to Spain looking for work.*

# CHAPTER 2

## *Contacting The Locals*

So you are here in Spain and no job so where do you start?

*Go contact the locals.*

The best source of jobs and **work in Spain** is the locals as they know who's who and who's hiring. I don't just mean the local Spanish people I mean the British community as well and these Brit expats normally know a lot about the area and just what sort of work is available and where to go.

When I first moved to Spain I was told of a local British club that met up every Monday night at a local British bar in town.

These local British clubs are in most towns so search for them and ask around.

So I went along on a Monday night and there was about 20 people all in this small bar at the end of town having a drink and chatting about life in Spain and just about everything else.

I was introduced to the Club secretary who ask me if I was living here and a little about myself, I told her that I was looking for work in Spain and she asked what I did for work. I told her that I was a carpenter and builder. Straight away she took me over to a Local guy who had been living in Spain for about 5 years and was building 2 new houses in the hills not far from here.

We started to chat and at the end of the evening he offered me a tryout with his guys working on 1 of these new houses. He told me that at the moment they needed brick layers not carpenters but they soon would need carpenters so if i could help out the 2 bricklayers they had I may be in luck for work as a carpenter later on.

As I was there only for a week as we were just looking for work I told him I would need to return to the Uk for 2 weeks to shut up my place and return here to rent. He said that would be great as they had only just started work on this house here.

He was not offering very good wages compared to what I had been earning in my home town of Brighton on the south coast of England but it was a start and at least I would be living in sunny Spain not cold wet England so i jumped at the offer.

The next day my then wife and I went and rented a 2 bed apartment in town near the beach for just 6 weeks to start as we still were in shock that I had found a job so quickly.

We left a case here with some cloths and returned to Brighton to collect a few things.

Just 2 weeks later we returned and I called this guy saying that I was here now and ready for work. He told me that a guy would pick me up that next Monday and that is how Found work in Spain.

Now I was very lucky or was I as I had looked into the area first and did some searches online and found that there was a local British club here. All this fell into place and made it easier for me to find this guy and acquire work in Spain.

These sort of British clubs are all over Spain and some are very different to others.

One I went to a few years later was in a main town and was very snooty and the people were very clicky and not that friendly to new people joining them who had not bought a house yet. This is not always the case though as many of these clubs are for people just like me who are straight off the boat so to speak and really don't know anything as many Brits that first move here.

These clubs are a great way to find out not just work here but where you get bills paid, best place to buy a second hand car and who can help you translate documents here. This is an important one when you are first here if you don't speak Spanish.

For about a year my wife and I went along to this club to meet up and chat to the locals and we made some great new friends here that after 16 years now I still see a few of them around now and then but personally I have stopped going as I found that once I had started work and got my new life set here and started speaking Spanish, I found the conversation a little boring as many of these Brits mostly stay in their own little groups and go places together and as many are retired here they have somewhat different lives to ours.

These are very helpful places to go even if you are not looking for work as they do have a wealth of local knowledge to share that's very handy if you get to know them.

Even if there's no clubs like that in your area there will be a more low key group of local expats that meet in some local bar each week just look around and you will find them and don't be afraid to go up and just start chatting to them they are nearly always very friendly people who could help you find that dream job in Spain.

Just make sure that you join some Spanish clubs too as this is where the real fun starts.

When I got divorced here about 4 years after moving here* *that's another book on its own* I joined several Spanish clubs here mostly to meet new friends like a walking club a climbing club and a dancing club. At all three of these clubs not only did I make new friends but got a lot of work from people that I met as well. It's all about reciprocity and getting people to know like and trust you then they will have you do work for them and recommend you to their family and friends. The more you put yourself out there the more these opportunities open up to you.

Last year there was a guy who had just moved to Spain with his wife and 2 daughters, he had been here about 3 months and at a local British bar I was introduced to him. I asked him if he was working and he told me that he would be going to look for work that next week as they had settled in well now in their new house here in town. He told me that he only needed to work about 3 days a week so I asked him what he was looking for .

He told me that he was going to work at a car rental company so I asked which one. He told me that he was not sure and he was just looking at the moment so I said that his Spanish must be pretty good then? Ah no he said just the basics. In Spain when a Brit says that it normally means very little too nothing. OK I said but how are you going to work there if you can't speak Very good Spanish and he replied that he was only going to rent just to the British.

I didn't know what to say at first as he was very serious, I told him that all the paperwork would have to be filled in in Spanish and that he would need to answer the phone and it would probably be Spanish people speaking Spanish, His reply was a strange aah yes.. I changed the subject as I could see that he hadn't thought about this one much.

He should have asked around as the locals would have told him this from day one.

Local people and the clubs are a key to finding work in Spain.

# CHAPTER 3

## *Wages In Spain*

One important thing you need to understand is that the wages here in Spain can be a lot lower than many European countries and way lower than that of England.

There is a counter side to this though, you don't need as much money as things are a lot cheaper here.

Below I will give you some idea of what people earn and what I have paid my staff in the past plus what I hear other British here are earning now.

Before I start shouting out numbers and earnings here let me just tell you some of the costs that I personally pay here and my cost of living to give you an idea of how you can live here and what you may need to earn.

I just paid my motor bike tax for the year and it was 8.50 Euros for the year, the road tax for each of my cars was 58 Euros a year. we paid council tax or the equivalent here of 130 a year and that includes them emptying the rubbish here every night at midnight not once a week like my mum's town in the UK.

Food and drink here is cheaper too with a small beer and free tapas here costing me 1.50 and when my wife and I go out at the weekends we normally have about 3 drinks each with food and that costs 18.Euros total. Here in Almeria the tapas are free. Another reason I moved to Almeria. See the history of the FREE Tapas click here.

I know a guy here who works 6 days a week at the local shopping center as maintenance and he works around 50 hours a week for 1800 a month.

Most office staff earn around 2200 a month and shop staff earn around 1000 a month.

Trade people earn more like my friend who is a plumber here he is Spanish and he earns about 3500 a month but he is self employed and works all hours.

Manual labor jobs are very low pay here and getting a contract job can be very hard as the bigger Spanish companies normally only take you on for 3 or 6 months at a time and this is because they can get shot of you easily and don't have to pay as much tax or benefits as for a full time contract.

When I first started here I was paid 300 Euros a week cash in hand and this is now illegal but some still do it. My wages went up to 375 a week after 1 year but I was made in charge so had more responsibility.

When I first went self employed here a few years later I was charging by the day and my day rate was 50 Euros a day. This stayed like this for several years as things were tuff here but the last few years I worked here I charged 100 a day.

If you come here and think you can make the same money as back in the UK then you will have a shock, you also have to compete with the local Spanish people and they are use to working for less and Spanish people will only pay as much as they have to even if you are brilliant and a very hard worker.

You may be able to charge the British more and I did this most of the time and heres why.

If the British are living here full time then most will not be able to speak enough Spanish to call out a plumber or electrician, so when I got a call for my building services I would contact my trades people and arrange for them to do the works so I needed to earn not just for my time but for my knowledge and this knowledge was being able to speak to them and knowing where to get the right help and materials from.

## 30 Euros for flicking a switch.

Last year I charged 30 Euros to turn on a switch on a boiler for a customer and here is why.

It was about 8pm and I got a call from a new British guy who had just moved here and bought a new apartment in town. He had no hot water and needed a plumber to come fix it. I arranged to go there and then to have a look so as I could see what I needed to tell my plumber to do.

Once I arrived I saw that it was a boiler that we fit here a lot and there was water but no hot water. I Told the guy that I could fix it there and then and it would be quick and would cost 30 Euros. He said great do it now then, so I reached up behind the boiler and flicked the reset button that had tripped out when they turned on the power. All worked and in 30 seconds he had hot water.

That's a lot to charge for that he said. I replied that he had called me out at night and I had to drive there so it cost me petrol and the job was completed fast with no mess and all was working fine, now he could have a hot shower. I explained that he was paying for my knowledge.

I didn't feel like I was ripping him off as if he could speak Spanish and called out a Spanish plumber for that night he would have had to wait and he would also be charged a lot more.

This later became one of my best clients here a few years later when he bought a house and needed it renovated as he still could not speak Spanish. This is a great market to get into when you can speak Spanish as you can work for both Brits and the Spanish.

But keep your prices low to start with and as they get to know like and trust you then you can start to charge a more normal price for your experience.

Many New Brits here start off trying to charge UK prices and may get a few Brits pay them but it won't last. There is always someone doing it cheaper here so if you want to work here as self employed you need to start off very competitive and build up as you get more clients and they appreciate your work.

# CHAPTER 4

## *Most popular Jobs For Expats In Spain*

There are a few popular jobs and ways people find **work in Spain** once they first move here and some are good and some not so much, now I will share what I have seen British people do for work here and how it has worked out for them.

### *Bar Work.*

Probably the most popular and first thought of is finding work in a bar here but this has good and bad sides so here goes..... The good side... Normally bar owners have several staff members who work shifts in the bars and this may fit in very well around your life here and the hours that you wish to work. Maybe you just need a few mornings a week to help pay for your tapas then this can be just the job for you.

You get to meet a load of new people and make many new friends and can hear of other opportunities as you are working in the bar that could lead to better work and wages for you.

Now the bad... wages are normally very low and paid in cash so you may be working here illegally. You may have to change your working hours to fit in around the bar and not your life so these hours can and do change often with little notice, not so good if you have a family and daily routine. If the bar is in a touristy area you will for sure get in a few loud badly behaved customers who could upset you.

Where I first lived here there was 3 local British bars that did all the usual British beers and English breakfasts and these bars all had a very high turnover of staff as working conditions are not normally that great. If you can get work in a Spanish bar you would need to speak very good Spanish or you will not last.

There is always bar work in the larger towns especially near the coast but remember that in the winter months even in Spain things go quiet and bars either close down or just down need the staff as much so this type of work is very hit and miss.

## Cleaning Jobs

Most British here who have a house normally get in cleaners about once or twice a week to do the daily clean through as the wages are low they can afford to do this here and the Spanish young girls or young mothers have this market sown up really.

I know of several British people who have built up some clients here and do make a decent living here cleaning other people's houses but it is hard dirty work.

Also If you can get in with local estate agents then cleaning of apartments for new arriving tourists can be another way to get regular work here if cleaning work is what you are looking for.

Many Spanish homes have cleaners in 2 times a week so if you could speak a little Spanish then this too could be for you.

**The Airport Runs**

In every town or village you will find some Brit doing the Airport Run.

This is when you take and collect people from the airport and drop them off at their loggings.

*THIS IS TOTALLY ILEGAL HERE.*

Several times on the Spanish TV I have seen police stopping English people dropping off people at the airport and checking all their papers, they are on the lookout for this here now and if the local taxis see you they have been known to smash up your car as well as lay into you.

They pay high rates to operate from the airports and don't like it when Brits do it on the quiet. They are also looking out for the same cars and faces at the airport and will take action I have seen it at Malaga airport a few years back.

Something else to remember if you do this is that your insurance does not cover you if you have a crash and in the case of a crash and the police are called your passengers will sell you out and you will be in trouble.

**Property Key holding and maintenance**

This is quiet a good one really and I know several people here who do this and do ok with it.

Property owners here who rent out their place when they are not here or owners who just want the place cleaned and ready for when they return give keys to trusted Brits living here and they look after the place.

There is a retired lady I know who

lives here that started off just holding the keys for a friends place and they recommended her to a few others and now she has almost a full time business here and has cleaners and people who help her and she is doing very well. Most of this work is cash and she probably is not declaring it but it would be very difficult to catch her out on this.

If you started as self employed here and did it the right way you could make a good living doing this and I personally know people here who do.

# CHAPTER 5

## *Papers You Need To Work In Spain*

To work and reside in Spain for more than **three months** it will be necessary for you to obtain a registration certificate. Printed official application form (EX-18), filled out and signed by the EU citizen.

A valid passport or national identity document.

Depending on the occupation of the foreign worker, the following documents should be presented:

If you are a foreign worker coming to work for a business in Spain you must present employers' contract, employment certificate or a work contract. If you are a self-employed worker you should submit any of the following documents, registration to social security, registration to the Census of Economic Activities or a mercantile registration.

You have to file a tax return if you're a Spanish resident and also if you're a non-resident. You can do this online now but Personally I find it best to just get a recommended accountant here who speaks English, there are a few around just asks or shop online..

At the bottom of this page I have a link to My old accountant who did my books here for several years and who now Is the chief of the British consulate here and has an accountants company with his brother.

You don't need to file a tax return if you earn less than €22,000 per year, as long as your entire income comes from one single source. However, you'll need to file if you think you've paid too much tax and want a refund.

There are two types of income in Spain: general income ( renta general ) and savings income ( renta del ahorro ).

**The General income** is all the money you have earned during the tax year. This includes your salary, employment benefits and business income.

This income is taxed at different rates, depending on how much you earned during the year. There are also a number of deductions you can make, resulting in less tax.

Claim for everything id did even my dog who i said was a guard dog for my business.

**Savings income** is any other income you may have. It includes interest, dividends and income from investments,

Including life insurance policies, as well as income from transfers of assets (capital gains). This income is taxed at fixed rates and you cannot make any deductions or allowances.

**Non-residents** are liable for tax on any income earned in Spain, such as a money deposit with a Spanish bank, a property in Spain or income derived from any business in Spain.

Property owners here are taxed on their property income. The tax base is the property catastral

value (valor catastral), which can be found on any IBI receipt. The cadastral value is calculated through the land and market value of your property, and the tax base rate is 24% of 2% of the cadastral value.

Should you fail to pay this tax, you will be charged and penalized by the Spanish Tax Agency if you try to sell your property. If you are a Spanish resident, you will be taxed for your worldwide income. Double tax treaties are in place to avoid double-taxation. If there is no treaty with your country of origin, you may deduct the foreign tax paid; foreign compensation may also be applied.

Your Spanish lawyer may calculate this amount for you.Non-residents living more than

six months (183 days) in Spain are also considered residents for tax purposes, even if they have not obtained their residence permit.

You will need to file your tax return for the previous calendar year during May or

June, and the overall deadline for submitting your return and paying outstanding tax is 30 June.

OK so it all sounds a bit complicated I know that's why you need to just get an accountant here and let him worry about it all. It still is not a nice day for me when i have to do this each year and I speak Spanish so if your Spanish is good or bad just go the easy rout and get your accountant to do it as it may save you worry and headaches in the long run.

Always get a recommendation from someone that you know who has been doing their books with as there are some accountants here that are just not that interested and they do drag on things and like to charge you for every little thing that they can.

As I stated before I had a very good accountant and he now has offices all over Spain and can put you in touch with the right people if he can't personally help you.

He is also the chief British Consulate here in Almeria and can answer any questions you may have.   Ask for him Personally and say **David Wright** sent you.

Here is his Website    **Alejandro.**

http://gestoriasalvador.com/en/consulado-honorario-britanico/

Here is his phone number    +34 950 2371 55

Spanish    Tax    questions    answered    here..
https://liveinalmeria.wordpress.com/

# CHAPTER 6

## *Your CV for Spain*

Having a good CV is important in the UK and here in Spain it's no different but there is something new that I have seen here and around the world that you may not have seen that could help you **find work in Spain**.

Your online CV...... **Wait** this is not just an online CV.

Condense your CV to make all your details fit on just one page of an A 4 paper.

Have a nice photo of you at the top and all the main details of your experience that you think may be of benefit here in Spain.

Keep it straight to the point and easy to read, then get it translated into Spanish.

**NOT Google translate get it done properly.**

I use Google translate a lot and its very good but there are some things that just don't translate that well and you could look like a twit even before you go for that interview.

Once you have your CV prepared in Spanish then you can start sending it out MY EMAIL. yes EMAIL not post.

Look at the places that you think you may like to work at and search online for them and there is always a number email or contact there so send it to them by Email. If not call them and ask for their email.

Send this email with an attachment . The attachment is your Cv.

In this email Just say that you have a photo of you and CV that you would like their opinion on.

Most people will be intrigued to see what you look like and most will open your email. Hopefully you are not butt ugly and scare them off, they should read it as its just one short page.

About 3 days later call them and ask to speak to the boss or someone in charge.

Ask them what they thought of your CV and if they may be interested. At this point have a copy of this email ready to send them there and then if they say they lost it or didn't read it then you can send it straight away and they have no excuses to not read it and be even more intrigued to find out just who you are.

If it doesn't get you an interview there and then ask them how you can improve that Cv so as to have a better chance next time. Most people will love to tell you how to do it their way and this can even change their mind about you and may give you a second chance, if not you could follow what they say to improve it either way you will come out better off.

Before I went self employed here I did do this several times and it did get me an interview as I attached a few photos of jobs that I had done in the carpenter business.

Always follow up on these emails a few days later don't leave it more than 5 days or they will forget you. With an online CV you could send these out in their hundreds even from your home in the Uk and you know it's all just a numbers game really, so the more you send out the better your chances. Most people though don't follow up with a call after and this can really be the deal breaker.

It has worked for me so why can't it work for you.

Just think that one interview could lead to a job in Spain and that could be all you need to get your new life off to a great start. Remember what I said about just getting one foot in first even if the job is not really what you want it's a start. This is just how I started here working hard long hours in the sun now I am sitting long hours on the beach.

# CHAPTER 7

## *Find Work In Spain Now*

In this chapter I will show you where you can start looking for work right now today.

Whether you are in Spain or the UK there are some places that you can search for jobs and post your CV now.

As above the local British papers printed in Spain are a great resources but there are a few others that most Brits don't know about so here they are.

Some of these are Spanish sites so if you can't understand them just use Google translate and copy and paste.

If you have the paper back version of this book then just type the urls into any web browser.

https://www.milanuncios.com/ofertas-de-empleo/

https://www.thinkspain.com/jobs-spain

https://www.thelocal.es/jobs/

http://www.jobsinbarcelona.es/

http://www.jobsinmadrid.es/

https://www.thelocal.es/

https://www.indeed.es/

https://www.reed.co.uk/jobs/jobs-in-spain

https://www.spotahome.com/blog/jobs-in-spain-for-english-speakers/

**A recon Trip**

If you have time off or have holiday due then why not go to Spain to look for work, now this is not going to be a holiday but a recon trip.

Why not book a recon trip to Spain. Once you know that area that you like and have done a bit of research, why not book a trip there. NOT A HOLIDAY but a fact finding trip just to see if it really is the place for you and use your time there to gather as much information as possible about the work prospects there.

This is not a trip where you get to lay on the beach and top up your tan, there will be loads of time for that once you have a steady job there and are earning a bit of money.

These fact finding trips should be from 3 to 5 days, that's all you need to get a good feel of the area and speak to the locals. This is the week that you will go to all the Brit bars and clubs you can just to chat with locals about what they think about your chances of finding work there, Just by asking them you may find that they have contacts there or know a guy who is looking for people just like you. Then you come back and plan out your return trip.

Its best to book these trips on your own, just a cheap flight and cheap accommodation as you are just going to be sleeping in the room not on holiday. You must stay focused and use all your time here to just concentrate on looking for work and putting out your CVs in as many places as possible.

There are some great last minute deals to be had if you know where you want to go wait till the last minute to book it for best prices and just go for it.

One my brother uses for his last minute trips here is ON THE BEACH .com.

Last month the 2 of them came here for £250 each, that's flights accommodation breakfast and transfers. This was in a 4 star hotel right on the beach as well.

Another friend of mine uses Airbnb. He paid £30 a night for an apartment in Barcelona.

Use my discount link.... Booking.com app and get €15 back with this coupon code: DAVIDI50 https://booking.com/s/73_4/davidi50

Make a list before you come to Spain of places to visit and British areas to see and meet people so as you can utilize your time here to the maximum.

If on your trip it really is not what you think or you didn't *find work in Spain* then that's cool, it just means that you found a place that's not right for you and you haven't spent too much money either. Then go home and plan another trip.

Remember that the areas of Spain that you may want to live long term may be harder to find work but if you go to a place that you are more likely to find work, then once you get work and start accustoming yourself to these new ways, you can think about moving to your dream location.

The first 2 years I worked here it was 1 hour drive away from where I really wanted to be and 1 hour each way every day in the mid summer months was not really what I wanted and the town where I worked was defiantly not where I wanted to be but it was a means to an end and worked out well for me in time.

Another thing to remember is the time of year you do these recon trips. don't go in the winter as many places tend to close down or are on a go slow so to speak in the winter months. Businesses tend to let staff go in the winter months so they will probably not be looking to take on new staff. Also in August most businesses have their Main holidays in August and shut down for the 4 weeks. This is famous here in all of Spain as you can't get anything done in August. It may be a good time if you are looking for bar work or in the tourist industry though. Remember this may only be seasonal though.

Also on your recon trip stay right in the center of things you don't want to have the expenses of hiring a car as most main places here now have very good and cheap public transport that is ok.

Personally this is what I did when I first came here and it worked out great.

We booked a last minute deal in a really cheap hostel near the beach and although it rained the first 2 days and we nearly got back on that plane, I did find work on my first trip here and on the last day as well. Most of this was not really luck as we had done a lot of online research weeks before and liked what we saw so did even more in-depth research on the area that paid off big time. Once we arrived we know the layout of the town and where we needed to go due to the fact that we had seen it all online.

You can now even search on Google earth and then go right into STREET VIEW and even read the signs of the streets so this will give you a great idea of what the place is like.

I even found the British club this way and saw it in Google street view, so when we were there we know just what to look for.

Facebook Groups is another great way to connect with People living where you want to live in Spain.

Just type in an area of Spain in groups and loads will come up. Come check out our Facebook Group **British Expats In Spain**..... https://www.facebook.com/groups/BritishExpatsInSpain/ Our group is set up to help people who are thinking of moving to Spain and has loads of great information like all the papers you need when moving to Spain.

There are always people in these groups that have an extensive first hand knowledge of the area and maybe contacts for work that are living in or around the area that you like and all you need to do is post a question and you will get a response in minutes. Also here is where you can ask them about where you should do your first recon trip and they will give you information about local accommodation.

Facebook groups are under the left hand side menu bar on your facebook profile and is you type in words or phrashes like...work in spain    jobs in spain    employment in spain ///words like these or combinations of words like these you will be shown a long list of groups that you can join and most of these groupd accept you straight away/

Some of these groups may ask you to answer a question that is easy and this is just showing that you are a real person not some robot spamming links in the group.

This also shows that the group is active and is being regulated by some one and so will be a better group to join/

Look for groups that have more than 500 members and that are being used as many groups you can see that the last post was made several days ago. if there is no body posting in the group every day then that group will not be very helpful to you so just move on to the next one as there are loads of them.

Also just join as many groups as you can and after a few days you will get to see what ones you like and many are just full of people posting stupid adds or rubbish items for sale. these groups will not help leave the group and move on.

Facebook will block , ban or mute you if you start posting in mulitple groups more than 3 or 4 a day and this ban is normally for a few days and has happened to me many times, dont worry too much wait a few days and start again.

To avoid this make sure that you like and comment on several post within that group before you start posting your questions or links.

# CHAPTER 8

## *Going Self Employed In Spain*

Is it worth it? ....Personally I say yes as there are pros and cons as I show below but at the end of the day I prefer to work for me the hours that I want and where I want and for who I want rather than work for a boss who tells you what to do. Read on and you decide....

Many people are now attracted by the opportunity to work from home doing something that they love to bring financial freedom and going self employed in Spain may be right for you. There are now many businesses and ways that you can work from home in Spain running a small business or even working online for a company.

**The pros** for an expat doing so are is that Spain already has a thriving self-employed sector, it's one of the largest in Europe with more than 3 million people. self-employed individuals Being self employed here is known as 'autónomos'.

However, despite the enthusiasm for self-employment in Spain it is not the easiest of countries to set up in business with their love of unnecessary paper work and it can be an expensive process just to become established and set up.

It is important to consider the legal arrangements you will need to meet for starting up a business, as well as taxes.

For those *moving to Spain* for self-employment from another EU country you can do so easily **but** you must register as self-employed, while those from outside of the European Union may need a visa to enter the country and they may also need a work permit.

We are all Still waiting to see what happens with the Brexit mess.

Everyone wishing to be self-employed must register for Social Security (Seguridad Social) and income tax at your local offices.

You will need to sort out your NIE numbers first though, The NIE is a number that defines an expat as living and working in Spain. Spanish people are issued with a similar number called a DNI. The NIE will enable them to work as an employee as well as being self-employed and also enable the opening of a bank account, or buying property and obtaining utilities.

There is all the information on documents you need when first moving to Spain and where to get it all from in **my first book** in the series **"Moving To Spain from dream to reality"** See it on Amazon or here. https://amzn.to/2Oionee

Once you are self employed you will then need to register with the tax authority (Agencia Tributaria or Hacienda) in Spain as self-employed. This can be done online or at the tax office.

**Among the cons** for self-employment in Spain is the hefty price autónomos have to pay in social security fees every month which add hugely to their running costs.

The standard amount being charged is currently €285 per month, but there are reductions available depending on the type of business and the situation of the individual, including their age and gender as well as how long they have been self-employed in their industry.

Remember though once self employed you can claim back all your expenses and I try to claim for everything I can and often get it accepted.

It is definitely worth hiring a good accountant to help with the paperwork I can recomend you mine, His name is Alejandro, just say David sent you heres his website.... http://gestoriasalvador.com/en/consulado-honorario-britanico/

In Spain the Social Security fee is paid every month regardless of how much the autónomo actually earns though they will need to earn the minimum wage of €9,173 annually.

It's also possible to pay a supplement to earn a higher pension and for sickness and accident cover while at work. For many self-employed people this is a worthwhile small fee. These figures may have change since writing this book so check first.

## Some Good News

Heres the good news though.... unlike many other countries the social security contribution does cover them for **healthcare and a pension**, as well as **unemployment and sick leave**. The rate of contribution is the same regardless of how much the expat is earning as self-employed though expats should appreciate that they are not entitled to some benefits, such as a pension, until they have paid contributions into the system for at least 15 years.

Also, to help expats become established in Spain, the 'tarifa plana' is a scheme that runs for around 18 months which sees the social security contributions for the expat starting with a small amount and gradually increasing to the full amount.

This system tends to be for autónomo men aged under 30 and for women under 35 though it's also possible for someone who hasn't registered under the scheme in the last five years to claim an 80% discount for the first six months.

The expat must charge IVA regardless of how much their annual turnover is; anyone supplying a service or goods which are subject to VAT/IVA will also need to file a return every quarter though their VAT bill doesn't have to paid until

January.

## Get the right help

Getting professional advice before becoming self-employed in Spain really will be money well spent. The tax system does change frequently and there are various incentives available to help people start up.

For many people **moving to Spain** the freedom of freelance life is worth the stresses. If you get a good accountant then you just let him worry about it all.

The process for registering as self-employed in Spain may appear daunting to expats who are really keen to work for themselves so many people tend to hire a gestor, or business manager, rather than an accountant, who can deal with the necessary paperwork and help smooth the path to becoming self employed..

The gestor can also process the expat's tax returns every quarter and this may be a sound investment since the rules on tax change regularly.

## Claim for everything I do.

When it comes to invoicing, the Spanish authorities have specific requirements and all autónomos must issue and keep copies of all invoices for the work they've done, and must also retain receipts if they are deducting expenses for tax purposes. The invoice itself can be in Spanish or English, both are acceptable, though many expats tend to use bilingual invoices.

Every relevant business expense can be deducted from your tax bill including the accountant's fees, office expenses, your cars used for work purposes. The self employed setting up fees can also be deducted, as can internet and phone services. I even claimed for my dog saying he was a guard dog as he was protecting my workshop where my tools were.

Going Self Employed Is in my personal view a very good idea and a great way to start working on your own here in Spain. It also gives you the freedom to work for others where and when you want and the hours that you like.

### Davids Tip After being self employed here 16 years.

If you are working for clients and need to go to their homes then the top tip is always be on time. So many Brits here work like the Spanish and if they say they will be with you at 10am that normally means about 10.30. It is not just the British that like you to be on time the Spanish like it too.

The Spanish are use to the Spanish workers saying manana and being late but when you are on time they really are shocked so make it a habit. I always ring them if I am going to be even 5 minutes late just to let them know and this goes down well with them.

Many of my repeat customers have called me just because they know I will come when I say I will and that my work and work ethic is always good. Many small jobs that I did for new customers I charged very little or on some occasions did for free just to get repeat work and it works.

One day a new customer called saying that a friend had recommended me and they just needed a door handle repaired as it kept getting stuck when they shut the door. This was an easy fix for me about 15 mins so I did it for free and gave them a business card. About a week later they called again and this time it was for a complete new kitchen, Worth doing the first job for free.

There are always bad customers as well and I had a few like ones who didn't want to pay. The first year I was self employed I had this Welsh Guy that I had just built a new garage for and he wanted the long garden wall painted both sides in white when we finished the garage. He paid me for the garage and I didn't take a deposit for the painting of the wall as it was only 400 Euros and he had paid it straight away.

When I finished the painting of the wall he said he was not

going to pay as it needed repairs as well. AS I tried to explain to him the quote I did was for just 2 coats of paint to the wall NO repairs but he started to get angry and said I should take him to court for the 400 Euros.

My accountant informed me that there was a small claims court I could go to and that as I had the quote with his signature on it I will win BUT... it may take 2 years to get it and it will cost me up to 300 Euros that I needed to pay upfront so I just decided to write it off.

Always give a written quote and get them to sign it and always get a deposit.

Normally this is how I work even for good regular customers as I feel if they dont want to pay a deposit they may be trouble at the end of the job.

Say the work I quoted for was 1000 Euros. I would ask for 1 3rd up front and then second payment when we arrived at the job to start and the balance at the end.

As a carpenter and builder my material cost would have to be paid for mostly even before I started the job so that's why I always get deposits. My brother just had double glazing fitted on his house in the UK and he had to pay all the money up front 6 weeks before they even came to do the job.

Personally I feel here in Spain if you make it 3 payments both parties are happy and this covers most costs so if they do not pay at the end of the job you only lose your labor costs.

There are many holidays and fiestas here in Spain and if you work for other people here they may just give you that day off and often without pay but being self employed you can work when you decide. Sometimes if I have a big job on I work all over the weekends if possible then have a week day off to sit on the beach with my wife as she has flexi days at her works. There are many great advantages to being self employed that for me out way the hassle of setting it up at first.

Finding **work in Spain** can be hard if you don't know what you are doing and don't Speak Spanish but even if your Spanish is poor there is always things and ways of getting work here that can suit you and your needs. If you follow some of these tips in this book and do your research first then you will have a better chance of Finding Work In Spain.

If the info in this book has been of help to you please give me a quick review on Amazon as it helps boost my book rankings and so I can keep the publishing costs down for others .

There is a New Book in this series Out Soon on Amazon check now see if it's out yet. And come chat with me and hundreds of other expats in Spain now at our FaceBook group...........

BritishExpatsInSpain...https://www.facebook.com/groups/Bri
tishExpatsInSpain/

# CHAPTER 9
## Work Online In Spain

People are very skeptical about people that say they make money
online and rightly so as there are many people out there just
pushing systems that promise you the world but will just not work
in long term.

A few years ago after struggling to earn much money online I
decided that I needed help and found an online training company
and went all the way from Spain to Miami to have a week's
training with them. There I meet with others from around the
world that were just like me, very keen to learn more and also
met many top earners that were making crazy money every day. It
soon showed me that these money makers were real and people
really did make money online but it was going to take time and a
lot of effort on my part.

I took courses in all aspects of marketing and promoting with the
top leaders of this company showing just what they did to
generate their online income  and how I could use these tips to
boost my online earnings.

Not everything works for everyone and even a great system will
have different results for different people as its all down to how
you promote and package it. The trick is to find something that
you like first *or why do it right* then find your own ways and
ideas on how to do it for best results and just try it for a while and

continue to tweak it as you go and if the results are not what you want after a few weeks then change and move on until you find that one thing that fits.

**Proof.**

Posting pictures of hundreds of dollars in your hand or you sitting in some hot car is no proof that you are making any money .

On my blog and on my Facebook group i will post proof photos of some of my earnings so as you can see that i am earning money online. But Also take a look at my travel page and posts to see just how i spend my online income as i prefer to show how i spend my money rather that just how much i am making. you can see that some of the trips i have are way above the norm so it is sort of proof that i am earning money rather than just showing figures. We all know what it costs to travel and how much a holiday might cost like the **6 weeks** i had in Mexico or the 3 weeks in Bora Bora .A few years ago I had a trip back to the UK to visit my mum and took 4 of my best Spanish friends with me and I arranged for a stretched limo and Champaign to take us from the airport to our hotel. these are the sort of things you can do when you are making good money and it feels great.

Yes it really is possible to earn money online from anywhere in the world and not just in Spain and its a great way to earn a little extra income or even a full time income.

We have all seen these people posting how they are making hundreds of dollars a day working online and 99% of them are fake but some are real and there are things that you can learn that will give you an online income.

Several years ago when work here in spain was hard for me i

started to learn internet marketing and wanted to get rich quick who doesn't right.. well after paying out hundreds of dollars into systems that i didn't know what i was doing or were making me any money i soon learned that i needed help and needed to learn the right way.

I paid for a course in internet marketing that showed me just how to start promoting the right way.

This was a learning course not how to make money but how to promote. Once you know the right way to promote products you can start earning money online.

The course showed me how to set up a blog web pages and how to go about promoting any product.

It would take years to learn how to become a full time internet marketer and build websites and create products to sell on these websites to generate an online income BUT there is a short cut.

SELL NOTHING...PROMOTE OTHER PEOPLES PRODUCTS...and let them pay you commissions for doing it.

**Like** who?

Well just for starters  Amazon... There are millions of products sold every day all around the world on Amazon and Amazon have branches in most countries around the world and you are not limited to just promoting in one country...Promote to the world.

## HOW?

## Join the Amazon Affiliate Program

The Affiliate Program method was pioneered by Amazon.com. To give you an idea of how this works in action, I'll describe

Amazon.com's program briefly.

You sign up as an affiliate on their site and are assigned an Associate's ID.

You can get links to any product that is being sold on Amazon and that link will be coded to your account.

You then take that link and past in anywhere on the internet that you like, lets say a blog and When the visitor clicks on this link, the Amazon.com web server is programmed so that the visitor will be sent to the webpage for that product. At the same time my Associate's ID will be recorded with the visitor's session ID (an arbitrary number assigned to each visitor every time he enters the site), so that if the visitor makes any purchases on that session, I will be credited with their purchase. You will earn a commission on anything that person buys going through your link not just the product it is linked to..

While every merchant chooses  his payment system, this is how Amazon.com currently works,

You dont need to have ever bought or used that product to promote it.

Personally i do promote the products that i buy if i like them. lets face it if you buy the product then theres a good chance others will right.

- If my visitor gets to the Amazon.com site, begins to browse around, and ends up buying another product i still get a commission.
- Payments are made quarterly, so long as the total commission due that quarter is more than a minimum amount.

**Win-Win**

One of the reasons affiliate programs are so popular is that that offer a win-win situation for both merchant and affiliate.

**Merchant Advantage**
The merchant's cost for advertising a particular product is limited (largely) to the percentage paid to an affiliate, and the merchant only has to pay when a purchase is actually made. This is much better than banner advertising, where the merchant pays whether or not any purchase occurs. In fact, the amount paid to an affiliate for a purchase through an affiliate link is probably only 10% to 20% of the cost of that sale through banner advertising (which charges in cost per 1000 banner views, CPM).

What's more, if your visitor likes Amazon.com, he is likely to go directly there the next time he wants to purchase a product and Amazon.com has potentially gained a customer for life. (Of course, if the same visitor uses another link on your site to purchase another product, you'll get credit for that purchase also.)

**What to promote?**

Personally I like to promote this that i like. Just last week I was in Sevilla and needed to use the small solar folding panel that i bought on Amazon last year so i went to the amazon site and found the link to that solar charger and took out my mobile phone and shot a 30 second video with me using the solar charger saying how handy it was.

I then uploaded that video to my YouTube channel along with the link to it in the description box below the video. Now that video is on youtube for the world to see and if someone likes it and clicks on that link it takes them straight to the Amazon website and that product and if they but it i earn a commission any time of day or night even when i am asleep in bed and that is a great feeling getting up in the mornings and seeing that you just earned money as you were asleep.

Once you have uploaded the video you can then copy that link to the video and post that video link online anywhere.

The best thing to do with these links is to start a blog...its easy and free to create a blog with wordpress or any of the other free blog platforms that are out there.

Start a blog and just post about the things that you like. whatever it is that you are interested in there will always be others interested in the same things so write about it and then in these blog posts you can post your links to products and then tell the world about your blog and start to get followers to your blog. thats called traffic and there are many ways to get more traffic to your blog to get more people to see your posts and see and click on your affiliate links to generate your income.

Amazon has all the training that you need and the answer to any question you have so its easy to get an account and an affiliate id with them and start promoting products straight away. The key to making money with Amazon is to post your links everywhere you can to get as many people as possible to see them to increase your chances of earning a commission.

### How Much Can I Make?

The Amazon commissions range from just a few pennies to hundreds of dollars it all depends on what you are promoting but dont think just about promoting high end products that cost a lot to get higher commissions. its better to have many lower commissions on many products as they soon start to add up and your chances of making more sales are with the lower end priced products.

### *Making Money Online With Books*

At the moment I have 2 books out on Amazon and 2 more on the way.

Writing a short eBook or paperback and selling it on Amazon is another great way to earn an online income and it will bring in regular income for life. Once you write a book it is there forever and will always earn you money and the more books you have the more you will earn.

You dont need to be a professional writer or even have a major best seller to earn good income online with books.

If you write a short book say 50 pages then upload it to Amazon you can also have that book as an E book that people can download and Kindle is a great way to let people buy it and download it through Amazon.

The 2 books that i have written are about Spain and they are both on Amazon as paperbacks and on Kindle through Amazon and were both easy to upload to Amazon as they have all the tools and training on how to do it.

What to write about

Again here its all down to you, what every you are interested in there will be others that are interested in the same so write about it make it your version and people will buy it. I promote my books through Amazon and kindle and on my blog facebook group and YouTube channel and am selling about 1 book a day at the moment . thats a commission every day even when i am sleeping it is working for me. The commissions are straight away you do need to wait 2 months for the first cheque but after that they are every month.

If you have been through something or experienced something then write about that for my I moved to Spain so one of my books was all about moving to Spain. There are endless subjects that you could write about and Amazon even shows you what people are interested in so why not add this to you ways of making money online. the more things that you have out there earning for you the more you will make.

## ClickBank

*This was one of my best earners and several times i have woken up in the morning and checked my account to see that I have made over 100 dollars commission as i was asleep and thats an amazing feeling. If you get a good job you will earn money but learn how to earn an online income and you will earn money all day and night for ever.*

### So what is ClickBank?

Clickbank is an online retailer with a global presence, secure payment processing, reliable tracking and payouts, and an extensive affiliate network.

Vendors can create and sell both digital products (such as ebooks, software, and membership programs) and physical goods through ClickBank.

Customers purchase those products through ClickBank's secure order form, which accepts credit cards and PayPal, and provides advanced fraud protection. They also provide live customer service and support to customers who need it!

With ClickBank's affiliate program, affiliates can promote vendors' products and earn huge commissions. Affiliates use a ClickBank-provided referral link called a HopLink to direct customers to the vendor's site. If a customer then purchases a product, the affiliate receives a percentage of the sale that is credited directly to their ClickBank account. Their platform features reliable tracking and commission payouts that are made on time, every time.

This system allows for vendors to focus on selling great quality, high converting products as affiliates help them scale their businesses to new heights - both earning big in the process!

If you're interested in becoming a ClickBank vendor or affiliate, just google them and open an account with them and watch their training its all free to get started.

Join their Affiliate program and start promoting products that you like.

As an affiliate, all you have to do is sign up for a ClickBank affiliate account and then start browsing their marketplace which lists all the available products from their partner vendors. Once you find a good product (we'll get into that in a moment), ClickBank will give you a unique "affiliate link" that points to the vendor's sales page. All you have to do then is make people buy through that link. You earn a commission for any sale made through your affiliate links.

## *WHY CLICKBANK?*

Clickbank is not alone in what they do. There are many similar affiliate networks (I list some at the end of this blog post). So why and when would you choose Clickbank over others? Here's a breakdown of the top advantages I have experience over the years i have used them...

:

Very high commissions: Most ClickBank products pay 70%+ commission. You read that right. So in that case, if you sell a $100 product, you earn $70. You might think that's way too high to be real, but it is. They're mainly able to do that because most of their products are digital, which means there are no "production" costs, "shipping" costs or any other costs that are usually associated with physical products, hence the high commissions.

They pay fast: As often as weekly or bi-weekly. Many affiliate networks pay on a NET 30 basis, which means they keep your money for 30 days after you've earned them. This can be a huge inconvenience and create cash flow problems especially if you're running paid traffic.

They're newbie friendly: Some affiliate networks are strict when it comes to accepting new affiliates. They're usually scared of fraudsters who can potentially jeopardize the network's relationships with their advertisers and vendors by using shady promotional techniques. While this cautiousness is generally a good thing, it also makes it hard for new affiliates to get into those networks. How can you start taking your baby steps and experimenting with things when you're not even allowed to promote any products?

Big variety of products: They have thousands of products available across about two dozen categories. That's a lot of niches, a lot of products and a lot of opportunities.

The biggest factors involved are the products you choose and how you promote them. many of the better products there have training links that the owners of that product show you what works best to generate the best income for you. these owners want you to earn more money fast as the more you earn the more they sell.

But if you're asking if it's possible to make money with Click Bank as an affiliate in general, then the answer is yes, definitely. I personally have earned several thousand dollars with them.

It's not uncommon to see people doing 3 figures daily on ClickBank. A typical sale earns you $15-$50 in commission. Say the average is $30. This means you need 4 sales a day to hit $100+. Seems doable, doesn't it? Depending on your level of expertise you could hit your first sale in days or months.

But if you're a complete newbie, it's not unrealistic to aim for your first sale in 2-3 months. From that point onwards, once you prove to yourself that it works, things become much easier.

Personally I find that training or learning products are the best as people always want to know stuff and are looking for ways to learn from writing a book to earning money theres a product there that has training so why not promote that as people love to know how to do things and will pay to learn.

One of my best earners was wind and solar power that i was passionate about and promoted designs on how to build wind and solar systems at home and these products earned me some nice cheques.

Go take a look and see what you may like to promote and how it fits in with you and your way of life. just imagine if you had say a blog about solar power and you started promoting these solar products and their links on your blog and youtube channel do you think that anyone else in the world may be interested?

Youtube is another way i have made money online and starting several youtube channels is easy and if you build up the channel and the followers then you can get youtube to place adverts on your videos and earn commissions on these adverts/

Just imaging you are promoting some Amazon product, lets say my solar charger that i promote and you have the link on your videos to that amazon charger to earn commission and you also have youtube adverts on that video earning you commission, thats more ways to earn with the same product and all on automatic once you set it up and it works 24 hours a day every day earning you money.

How to promote your links faster and to a bigger audience
**Fiverr .com**

Fiverr , is a great site that you can get people to promote your business products and links for just a fiver and gets geat results and generates more traffic to any links. I use this site a lot as its cheap and they do the work fast normally in a few days and you see results straight away.

You can get people to create a video for you or a sound clip to help promote your links or just have them promote your links to their list of members or websites. they offer many amazing services and you can get things done that you dont know how to do or dont want to all for a small fee.

There are many sites out there like this but this is one of the better ones and there are also better services here that you can pay a little more for all in one place.

In the past i have used this website to generate more traffic to my blog and posts so as more people see my affiliate links and therefore more people but my products/ take a look and see what you can do.

Personally i normally chose people who are top sellers on this site or who have good reviews as they are most lickly to get you the best results.

Start off cheap and try a few out as its not expensive to see what works for you then you can scale it up once you see what works.

On my blog i also have a side bar where i post a photo or link to products of interest in the article . Say you post an article on your blog about a trip you just had to spain or the beach and that you used your solar charger there then post that link or even the video you made in the post or in te side bar so that people can see it. its all more ways of getting eyes on these products and chances or earning money from them. It's all really a numbers game and the more effort you put into promoting these affiliate links the more you will make. Be patient it all takes time, the things you do now sometimes take weeks or months to start seeing the results but then its there for ever.

There are many ways to start earning money online and here i have shown a few that i use but it does take hard work to start and you do have to put in the effort and it will take time but that time is going to pass anyway so why not start trying now and see what works for you.

## Davids Online Video Training Page

Here is the link to my private Video Training Page and the Password to Enter is ( **borabora**) its only for people who bought this book so please dont share.

https://britishexpatsinspain.com/video-training

### *This Is The End Of this Book*

### *But The beginning of your New and Exciting new adventure in Spain*

### *Now go make your dreams come true.*

David Wright

Printed in Great Britain
by Amazon